PROSPERITY
Promises

Kenneth Copeland

KCP Publications
Fort Worth, Texas

Prosperity Promises

ISBN 0-88114-731-1   # 30-0028

© 1985 Kenneth Copeland Ministries, Inc.

Unless otherwise indicated, all Scripture quotations are from the KING JAMES VERSION.

Published by KCP Publications
Fort Worth, Texas 76192

Text of the King James Version appears in boldface type.

The Amplified Bible . . . . Amp

The Bible: A New Translation (James Moffatt)

. . . . Mof

The New English Bible . . . . NEB

Our concept of prosperity must be broadened and deepened. We have kept our ideas confined to money and things that pertain to personal wealth, not realizing that God's laws of prosperity govern everything.

To prosper means to thrive or be successful. Prosperity means to advance or gain in anything good or desirable. It also means well-being. When we finally realize that our giving is the base and connection we have with God in *every* area of our lives, then *every* area of our lives will begin to prosper.

Second Corinthians 9:8-10 reveals that our giving increases the fruits of our righteousness, our right relationship with God. It increases the fruit of healing, the fruit of deliverance, our receiving from God in every area that righteousness has anything to do with. I am convinced that we have only barely scratched the surface in ministry, in the gifts of the Spirit, divine healing, preaching, finances and everything else the body of Christ has been promised through Jesus. I am also convinced that one of the main reasons we have continually fallen short of what is ours is not realizing it was all directly connected to our giving.

Giving has been a sideline instead of the main line of our lives. We've been working for a living and giving what we could. Ephesians 4:28 tells us to work so we will have seed to give. God intends for His people to live off their giving in His abundance instead of being limited by what they can earn or by what some welfare agency or pension doles out to them.

This book will help you meditate the scriptures on prosperity from God. Read it. Meditate on it. Carry it with you. Bathe your spirit and mind on these exceeding great and precious promises, and they'll cause you to partake of the divine nature of God. That in itself is to greatly prosper.

Jesus is Lord,

Kenneth Copeland

Kenneth Copeland

The above was taken from a letter written by Kenneth Copeland to his Covenant Partners.

Prosperity Scriptures

Psalm 35:27
Let them shout for joy, and be glad, that favour my righteous cause: yea, let them say continually, Let the Lord be magnified, which hath pleasure in the prosperity of his servant.

Amp—Let those who favor my righteous cause and have pleasure in my uprightness shout for joy and be glad, and say continually, Let the Lord be magnified, Who takes pleasure in the prosperity of His servant.

Mof—But may they shout for joy, may they be glad, who love to see me righted! May they have ever cause to say, "All hail to the Eternal, who loves to see his servant prospering!"

NEB—But let all who would see me righted shout for joy, let them cry continually, 'All glory to the Lord who would see his servant thrive!'

Genesis 13:2,5,6,14-17

And Abram was very rich in cattle, in silver, and in gold...And Lot also, which went with Abram, had flocks, and herds, and tents. And the land was not able to bear them, that they might dwell together: for their substance was great, so that they could not dwell together... And the Lord said unto Abram, after that Lot was separated from him, Lift up now thine eyes, and look from the place where thou art northward, and southward, and eastward, and westward: For all the land which thou seest, to thee will I give it, and to thy seed for ever. And I will make thy seed as the dust of the earth: so that if a man can number the dust of the earth, then shall thy seed also be numbered. Arise, walk through the land in the length of it and in the breadth of it; for I will give it unto thee.

Amp—Now Abram was extremely rich in livestock and in silver and in gold...But Lot, who went with Abram, also had flocks and herds and tents. Now the land was not able to nourish and support them so they might dwell together, for their possessions were too great for them to live together. The Lord said to Abram, after Lot had left him, Lift up now your eyes, and look from the place where you are, northward and southward and eastward and westward; For all the land which you see I will give to you and to your posterity for ever. And I will make your descendants as the dust of the earth, so that if a man can count the dust of the earth, then shall your descendants also be counted. Arise, walk through the land, the length of it and the breadth of it, for I will give it to you.

Mof—Abram was very rich in cattle, silver and gold...Lot, who accompanied Abram, also had flocks and herds and tents. Now the country could not support them both together; their possessions were so large that they could not live side by side...After Lot had parted from him, the Eternal said to Abram, "Look abroad now from where you are, north, south, east, and west; the land you see, I give it all to you and to your descendants for all time. I will make your descendants as numerous as the dust on the ground, so that if the dust of the ground could be counted your descendants could be counted. Up, traverse the length and breadth of the land, for I give it to you."

NEB—Abram was now very rich in cattle and in silver and gold...Now Lot was travelling with Abram, and he too possessed sheep and cattle and tents. The land could not support them both together; for their livestock were so numerous that they could not settle in the same district...After Lot and Abram had parted, the Lord said to Abram, 'Raise your eyes and look into the distance from the place where you are, north and south, east and west. All the land you can see I will give to you and to your descendants for ever. I will make your descendants countless as the dust of the earth; if anyone could count the dust upon the ground, then he could count your descendants. Now go through the length and breadth of the land, for I give it to you.'

Genesis 14:22,23
And Abram said to the king of Sodom, I have lift up mine hand unto the Lord, the most high God, the possessor of heaven and earth, That I will not take from a thread even to a shoelatchet, and that I will not take any thing that is thine, lest thou shouldest say, I have made Abram rich.

Amp—But Abram said to the king of Sodom, I have lifted up my hand and sworn to the Lord, God Most High, the possessor and maker of heaven and earth, That I would not take a thread or a shoelace or anything that is yours, lest you should say, I have made Abram rich.

Mof—Abram answered the king of Sodom, "By this hand raised to the Eternal, God Most High, Creator of heaven and earth, I swear I will not take a thread or string of yours! I will not have you say that, 'I made Abram rich.' "

NEB—But Abram said to the king of Sodom, 'I lift my hand and swear by the Lord, God Most High, creator of heaven and earth: not a thread or a shoe-string will I accept of anything that is yours. You shall never say, "I made Abram rich." '

Genesis 17:5-7

Neither shall thy name any more be called Abram, but thy name shall be Abraham; for a father of many nations have I made thee. And I will make thee exceeding fruitful, and I will make nations of thee, and kings shall come out of thee. And I will establish my covenant between me and thee and thy seed after thee in their generations for an everlasting covenant, to be a God unto thee, and to thy seed after thee.

Amp—Nor shall your name any longer be Abram (high father), but your name shall be Abraham (father of a multitude); for I have made you the father of many nations. And I will make you exceedingly fruitful, and I will make nations of you, and kings shall come from you. And I will establish My covenant between Me and you and your descendants after you throughout their generations for an everlasting, solemn pledge to be a God to you and to your posterity after you.

Mof—No longer shall your name be Abram, but Abraham (Many-father), for I have appointed you to be the father of many a nation; I will make you most fruitful, I will make nations out of you, and kings shall spring from you. And I will ratify my compact for all time, between me and yourself and your descendants from generation to generation, engaging to be a God to you and to your descendants after you.

5

NEB—Your name shall no longer be Abram, your name shall be Abraham, for I make you father of a host of nations. I will make you exceedingly fruitful; I will make nations out of you, and kings shall spring from you. I will fulfil my covenant between myself and you and your descendants after you, generation after generation, an everlasting covenant, to be your God, yours and your descendants after you.

Genesis 26:12-14
Then Isaac sowed in that land, and received in the same year an hundredfold: and the Lord blessed him. And the man waxed great, and went forward, and grew until he became very great: for he had possession of flocks, and possession of herds, and great store of servants: and the Philistines envied him.

Amp—Then Isaac sowed seed in that land, and received in the same year 100 times as much as he had planted, and the Lord favored him with blessings. And the man became great, and gained more and more until he became very wealthy and distinguished; He owned flocks, herds, and a great supply of servants, and the Philistines envied him.

Mof—Isaac sowed a crop in that country and reaped in the same year a hundredfold. The Eternal blessed him; he grew rich and increased till he became very rich, with property in flocks and herds and a large household. The Philistines became jealous of him.

NEB—Isaac sowed seed in that land, and that year he reaped a hundredfold, and the Lord blessed him. He became more and more powerful, until he was very powerful indeed. He had flocks and herds and many slaves, so that the Philistines were envious of him.

Genesis 30:43
And the man increased exceedingly, and had much cattle, and maidservants, and menservants, and camels, and asses.

Amp—Thus the man increased and became exceedingly rich, and had many sheep and goats, and maidservants, menservants, camels, and donkeys.

Mof—Who grew extremely rich, with large flocks, male and female slaves, camels, and asses.

NEB—So Jacob increased in wealth more and more until he possessed great flocks, male and female slaves, camels, and asses.

Genesis 39:2,3
And the Lord was with Joseph, and he was a prosperous man; and he was in the house of his master the Egyptian. And his master saw that the Lord was with him, and that the Lord made all that he did to prosper in his hand.

Amp—But the Lord was with Joseph, and he [though a slave] was a successful and prosperous man; and was in the house of his master the Egyptian. And his master saw that the Lord was with him, and that the Lord made all that he did to flourish and succeed in his hand.

Mof—But the Eternal was with Joseph, and he prospered; he was kept inside the household of his master the Egyptian, and his master noticed that the Eternal was with him, and that the Eternal prospered everything he took in hand.

NEB—The Lord was with Joseph and he prospered. He lived in the house of his Egyptian master, who saw that the Lord was with him and was giving him success in all that he undertook.

Exodus 3:7,8
And the Lord said, I have surely seen the affliction of my people which are in Egypt, and have heard their cry by reason of their taskmasters; for I know their sorrows; And I am come down to deliver them out of the hand of the Egyptians, and to bring them up out of that land unto a good land and a large, unto a land flowing with milk and honey; unto the place of the Canaanites, and the Hittites, and the Amorites, and the Perizzites, and the Hivites, and the Jebusites.

Amp—And the Lord said, I have surely seen the affliction of My people who are in Egypt, and have heard their cry because of their taskmasters and oppressors; for I know their sorrows and sufferings and trials. And I have come down to deliver them out of the hand and power of the Egyptians, and to bring them up out of that land to a land good and large, a land flowing with milk and honey—a land of plenty; to the place of the Canaanite, the Hittite, the Amorite, the Perizzite, the Hivite, and the Jebusite.

Mof—The Eternal said, "I have indeed seen the distress of my people in Egypt, I have heard them wailing under their slave-drivers; for I know their sorrows and I have come down to rescue them from the Egyptians and to bring them out of that land to a fine, large land, abounding in milk and honey, the country of the Canaanites, the Hittites, the Amorites, the Perizzites, the Hivites, and the Jebusites."

NEB—The Lord said, 'I have indeed seen the misery of my people in Egypt. I have heard their outcry against their slave-masters. I have taken heed of their sufferings, and have come down to rescue them from the power of Egypt, and to bring them up out of that country into a fine, broad land; it is a land flowing with milk and honey, the home of the Canaanites, Hittites, Amorites, Perizzites, Hivites, and Jebusites.'

Deuteronomy 8:18
But thou shalt remember the Lord thy God: for it is he that giveth thee power to get wealth, that he may establish his covenant which he sware unto thy fathers, as it is this day.

Amp—But you shall (earnestly) remember the Lord your God; for it is He Who gives you power to get wealth, that He may establish His covenant which He swore to your fathers, as at this day.

Mof—You must remember the Eternal your God, for it is he who gives you the power of gaining wealth, that he may ratify the compact which he swore to your fathers, as it is today.

NEB—But remember the Lord your God; it is he that gives you strength to become prosperous, so fulfilling the covenant guaranteed by oath with your forefathers, as he is doing now.

Deuteronomy 28:11
And the Lord shall make thee plenteous in goods, in the fruit of thy body, and in the fruit of thy cattle, and in the fruit of thy ground, in the land which the Lord sware unto thy fathers to give thee.

Amp—And the Lord shall make you have a surplus of prosperity, through the fruit of your body, of your livestock, and of your ground, in the land which the Lord swore to your fathers to give you.

Mof—The Eternal will make you overflow with prosperity in the fruit of your body, of your cattle, and of your ground, the ground that the Eternal swore to your fathers that he would give you.

NEB—The Lord will make you prosper greatly in the fruit of your body and of your cattle, and in the fruit of the ground in the land which he swore to your forefathers to give you.

Isaiah 1:19
If ye be willing and obedient, ye shall eat the good of the land.

Amp—If you are willing and obedient, you shall eat the good of the land.

Mof—If only you are willing to obey, you shall feed on the best of the land.

NEB—Obey with a will, and you shall eat the best that earth yields.

Joshua 1:8
This book of the law shall not depart out of thy mouth; but thou shalt meditate therein day and night, that thou mayest observe to do according to all that is written therein: for then thou shalt make thy way prosperous, and then thou shalt have good success.

Amp—This book of the law shall not depart out of your mouth, but you shall meditate on it day and night, that you may observe and do according to all that is written in it; for then you shall make your way prosperous, and then you shall deal wisely and have good success.

Mof—This lawbook you shall never cease to have on your lips; you must pore over it day and night, that you may be mindful to carry out all that is written in it, for so shall you make your way prosperous, so shall you succeed.

NEB—This book of the law must ever be on your lips; you must keep it in mind day and night so that you may diligently observe all that is written in it. Then you will prosper and be successful in all that you do.

Deuteronomy 29:9
Keep therefore the words of this covenant, and do them, that ye may prosper in all that ye do.

Amp—Therefore keep the words of this covenant, and do them, that you may deal wisely and prosper in all that you do.

Mof—Keep the terms of this compact, then, obey them, that you may succeed in all you undertake.

NEB—You shall observe the provisions of this covenant and keep them so that you may be successful in all you do.

Isaiah 55:11
So shall my word be that goeth forth out of my mouth: it shall not return unto me void, but it shall accomplish that which I please, and it shall prosper in the thing whereto I sent it.

Amp—So shall My word be that goes forth out of My mouth; it shall not return to Me void—without producing any effect, useless—but it shall accomplish that which I please and purpose, and it shall prosper in the thing for which I sent it.

Mof—So with the promise that has passed my lips: it falls not fruitless and in vain, but works out what I will, and carries out my purpose.

NEB—So shall the word which comes from my mouth prevail; it shall not return to me fruitless without accomplishing my purpose or succeeding in the task I gave it.

Psalm 37:25, 26
I have been young, and now am old; yet have I not seen the righteous forsaken, nor his seed begging bread. He is ever merciful, and lendeth; and his seed is blessed.

Amp—I have been young and now am old, yet have I not seen the [uncompromisingly] righteous forsaken or his seed begging bread. All day long he is merciful and deals graciously; he lends, and his offspring is blessed.

Mof—I have been young and I am old, but never have I seen good men forsaken; they always have something to give away, something wherewith to bless their families.

NEB—I have been young and am now grown old, and never have I seen a righteous man forsaken. Day in, day out, he lends generously, and his children become a blessing.

Proverbs 10:22
The blessing of the Lord, it maketh rich, and he addeth no sorrow with it.

Amp—The blessing of the Lord, it makes [truly] rich, and He adds no sorrow with it, neither does toiling increase it.

Mof—'Tis the Eternal's blessing that brings wealth, and never does it bring trouble as well.'

NEB—The blessing of the Lord brings riches and he sends no sorrow with them.

Proverbs 22:7
The rich ruleth over the poor, and the borrower is servant to the lender.

Amp—The rich rules over the poor, and the borrower is servant to the lender.

Mof—The rich rule over the poor, and the borrower is a slave to the lender.

NEB—The rich lord it over the poor; the borrower becomes the lender's slave.

Proverbs 19:17
He that hath pity upon the poor lendeth unto the Lord; and that which he hath given will he pay him again.

Amp—He who has pity on the poor lends to the Lord, and that which he has given He will repay to him.

Mof—He who cares for the poor is lending to the Eternal, and for his kindness he shall be repaid.

NEB—He who is generous to the poor lends to the Lord; he will repay him in full measure.

Luke 12:15
And he said unto them, Take heed, and beware of covetousness: for a man's life consisteth not in the abundance of the things which he possesseth.

Amp—And He said to them, Guard yourselves and keep free from all covetousness—the immoderate desire for wealth, the greedy longing to have more; for a man's life does not consist and is not derived from possessing overflowing abundance, or that which is over and above his needs.

Mof—Then he said to them, ''See and keep clear of covetousness in every shape and form, for a man's life is not part of his possessions because he has ample wealth.''

NEB—Then he said to the people, 'Beware! Be on your guard against greed of every kind, for even when a man has more than enough, his wealth does not give him life.'

Luke 12:21
So is he that layeth up treasure for himself, and is not rich toward God.

Amp—So it is with him who continues to lay up and hoard possessions for himself, and is not rich [in his relation] to God—this is how he fares.

Mof—So fares the man who lays up treasure for himself, instead of gaining the riches of God.

NEB—That is how it is with the man who amasses wealth for himself and remains a pauper in the sight of God.

Proverbs 28:13
He that covereth his sins shall not prosper: but whoso confesseth and forsaketh them shall have mercy.

Amp—He who covers his transgressions will not prosper, but whoever confesses and forsakes his sins shall obtain mercy.

Mof—He who covers up his sins shall never prosper; he who confesses and forsakes them is forgiven.

NEB—Conceal your faults, and you will not prosper; confess and give them up, and you will find mercy.

Psalm 1:3
And he shall be like a tree planted by the rivers of water, that bringeth forth his fruit in his season; his leaf also shall not wither; and whatsoever he doeth shall prosper.

Amp—And he shall be like a tree firmly planted [and tended] by the streams of water, ready to bring forth his fruit in its season; his leaf also shall not fade or wither, and everything he does shall prosper [and come to maturity].

Mof—He is like a tree planted by a stream, that bears fruit in due season, with leaves that never fade; whatever he does, he prospers.

NEB—He is like a tree planted beside a watercourse, which yields its fruit in season and its leaf never withers: in all that he does he prospers.

Proverbs 13:22
A good man leaveth an inheritance to his children's children: and the wealth of the sinner is laid up for the just.

Amp—A good man leaves an inheritance [of moral stability and goodness] to his children's children, and the wealth of the sinner [finds its way eventually] into the hands of the righteous, for whom it was laid up.

Mof—A pious man leaves wealth to his children's children: the sinner lays up treasure—to enrich the good!

NEB—A good man leaves an inheritance to his descendants, but the sinner's hoard passes to the righteous.

Hebrews 11:6
But without faith it is impossible to please him: for he that cometh to God must believe that he is, and that he is a rewarder of them that diligently seek him.

Amp—But without faith it is impossible to please and be satisfactory to Him. For whoever would come near to God must (necessarily) believe that God exists and that He is the Rewarder of those who earnestly and diligently seek Him (out).

Mof—And apart from faith it is impossible to satisfy him, for the man who draws near to God must believe that he exists and that he does reward those who seek him.

NEB—And without faith it is impossible to please him; for anyone who comes to God must believe that he exists and that he rewards those who search for him.

Mark 4:19
And the cares of this world, and the deceitfulness of riches, and the lusts of other things entering in, choke the word, and it becometh unfruitful.

Amp—Then the cares and anxieties of the world, and distractions of the age, and the pleasure and delight and false glamour and deceitfulness of riches, and the craving and passionate desire for other things creep in and choke and suffocate the Word, and it becomes fruitless.

Mof—But the worries of the world and the delight of being rich and all the other passions come in to choke the word; so it proves unfruitful.

NEB—But worldly cares and the false glamour of wealth and all kinds of evil desire come in and choke the word and it proves barren.

Luke 6:38
Give, and it shall be given unto you; good measure, pressed down, and shaken together, and running over, shall men give into your bosom. For with the same measure that ye mete withal it shall be measured to you again.

Amp—Give, and [gifts] will be given you, good measure, pressed down, shaken together and running over will they pour into [the pouch formed by] the bosom [of your robe and used as a bag]. For with the measure you deal out—that is, with the measure you use when you confer benefits on others—it will be measured back to you.

Mof—Give, and you will have ample measure given you—they will pour into your lap measure pressed down, shaken together, and running over; for the measure you deal out to others will be dealt back to yourselves.

19

NEB—Give, and gifts will be given you. Good measure, pressed down, shaken together, and running over, will be poured into your lap; for whatever measure you deal out to others will be dealt to you in return.

2 Corinthians 9:6
But this I say, He which soweth sparingly shall reap also sparingly; and he which soweth bountifully shall reap also bountifully.

Amp—[Remember] this: he who sows sparingly and grudgingly will also reap sparingly and grudgingly, and he who sows generously and that blessings may come to someone, will also reap generously and with blessings.

Mof—Mark this: he who sows sparingly will reap sparingly, and he who sows generously will reap a generous harvest.

NEB—Remember: sparse sowing, sparse reaping; sow bountifully, and you will reap bountifully.

Proverbs 3:9,10
Honour the Lord with thy substance, and with the firstfruits of all thine increase: So shall thy barns be filled with plenty, and thy presses shall burst out with new wine.

Amp—Honor the Lord with your capital and sufficiency [from righteous labors], and with the first fruits of all your income; So shall your storage places be filled with plenty, and your vats be overflowing with new wine.

Mof—Honour the Eternal with your wealth, and with the best of all you make; so shall your barns be full of corn, your vats brim over with new wine.

NEB—Honour the Lord with your wealth as the first charge on all your earnings; then your granaries will be filled with corn and your vats bursting with new wine.

Malachi 3:10-12
Bring ye all the tithes into the storehouse, that there may be meat in mine house, and prove me now herewith, saith the Lord of hosts, if I will not open you the windows of heaven, and pour you out a blessing, that there shall not be room enough to receive it. And I will rebuke the devourer for your sakes, and he shall not destroy the fruits of your ground; neither shall your vine cast her fruit before the time in the field, saith the Lord of hosts. And all nations shall call you blessed: for ye shall be a delightsome land, saith the Lord of hosts.

Amp—Bring all the tithes—the whole tenth of your income—into the storehouse, that there may be food in My house, and prove Me now by it, says the Lord of hosts, if I will not open the windows of Heaven for you and pour you out a blessing, that there shall not be room enough to receive it. And I will rebuke the devourer [insects and plagues] for your sakes, and he shall not destroy the fruits of your ground; neither shall your vine drop its fruit before the time in the field, says the Lord of hosts. And all nations shall call you happy and blessed; for you shall be a land of delight, says the Lord of hosts.

Mof—If you would enjoy ample rations in my House, then pay all your tithes into the treasury, and see what I will do, says the Lord of hosts; see if I will not then open the very sluices of heaven to pour a blessing down for you, a harvest more than enough; I will stop the locust from spoiling your crops, and your vines shall not miscarry (the Lord of hosts declares); all nations shall call you happy, the Lord of hosts declares, for you shall be a land of delight.

NEB—Bring the tithes into the treasury, all of them; let there be food in my house. Put me to the proof, says the Lord of Hosts, and see if I do not open windows in the sky and pour a blessing on you as long as there is need. I will forbid pests to destroy the produce of your soil or make your vines barren, says the Lord of Hosts. All nations shall count you happy, for yours shall be a favoured land, says the Lord of Hosts.

Hebrews 7:8
And here men that die receive tithes; but there he receiveth them, of whom it is witnessed that he liveth.

Amp—Furthermore, here [in the Levitical priesthood] tithes are received by men who are subject to death; while there [in the case of Melchizedek], they are received by one of whom it is testified that he lives [perpetually].

Mof—Again, it is mortal men in the one case who receive tithes, while in the other it is one of whom the witness is that 'he lives.'

NEB—Again, in the one instance tithes are received by men who must die; but in the other, by one whom Scripture affirms to be alive.

2 Corinthians 9:8,11
And God is able to make all grace abound toward you; that ye, always having all sufficiency in all things, may abound to every good work...Being enriched in every thing to all bountifulness, which causeth through us thanksgiving to God.

Amp—And God is able to make all grace (every favor and earthly blessing) come to you in abundance, so that you may always and under all circumstances and whatever the need, be self-sufficient—possessing enough to require no aid or support and furnished in abundance for every good work and charitable donation...Thus you will be enriched in all things and in every way, so that you can be generous, [and your generosity as it is] administered by us will bring forth thanksgiving to God.

Mof—God is able to bless you with ample means, so that you may always have quite enough for any emergency of your own and ample besides for any kind act to others...You will be enriched on all hands, so that you can be generous on all occasions, and your generosity, of which I am the agent, will make men give thanks to God.

NEB—And it is in God's power to provide you richly with every good gift; thus you will have ample means in yourselves to meet each and every situation, with enough and to spare for every good cause...And you will always be rich enough to be generous. Through our action such generosity will issue in thanksgiving to God.

Ecclesiastes 11:1
Cast thy bread upon the waters: for thou shalt find it after many days.

Amp—Cast your bread upon the waters, for you will find it after many days.

Mof—Trust your goods far and wide at sea, till you get good returns after a while.

NEB—Send your grain across the seas, and in time you will get a return.

3 John 2
Beloved, I wish above all things that thou mayest prosper and be in health, even as thy soul prospereth.

Amp—Beloved, I pray that you may prosper in every way and [that your body] may keep

24

well, even as [I know] your soul keeps well and prospers.

Mof—Beloved, I pray you may prosper in every way and keep well—as indeed your soul is keeping well.

NEB—My dear Gaius, I pray that you may enjoy good health, and that all may go well with you, as I know it goes well with your soul.

Matthew 6:25,26,28,30,32,33
Therefore I say unto you, Take no thought for your life, what ye shall eat, or what ye shall drink; nor yet for your body, what ye shall put on. Is not the life more than meat, and the body than raiment? Behold the fowls of the air: for they sow not, neither do they reap, nor gather into barns; yet your heavenly Father feedeth them. Are ye not much better than they?...And why take ye thought for raiment? Consider the lilies of the field, how they grow; they toil not, neither do they spin...Wherefore, if God so clothe the grass of the field, which today is and to morrow is cast into the oven, shall he not much more clothe you, O ye of little faith?...(For after all these things do the Gentiles seek:) for your heavenly Father knoweth that ye have need of all these things. But seek ye first the kingdom of God, and his righteousness; and all these things shall be added unto you.

Amp—Therefore I tell you, stop being perpetually uneasy (anxious and worried) about your life, what you shall eat or what you shall drink, and about your body, what you shall put on. Is not life greater [in quality] than food, and the body [far above and more excellent] than clothing? Look at the birds of the air; they neither sow nor reap nor gather into barns, and yet your heavenly Father keeps feeding them. Are you not worth more than they?....And why should you be anxious about clothes? Consider the lilies of the field and learn thoroughly how they grow; they neither toil nor spin...But if God so clothes the grass of the field, which today is alive and green and tomorrow is tossed into the furnace, will He not much more surely clothe you, O you men with little faith?....For the Gentiles (heathen) wish for and crave and diligently seek after all these things; and your heavenly Father well knows that you need them all. But seek for (aim at and strive after) first of all His kingdom, and His righteousness [His way of doing and being right], and then all these things taken together will be given you besides.

Mof—Therefore I tell you, never trouble about what you are to eat or drink in life, nor about what you are to put on your body; surely life means more than food, surely the body means more than clothes! Look at the wild birds; they sow not, they reap not, they gather nothing in granaries, and yet your heavenly Father feeds them. Are you not worth more than birds?....And why should you trouble over clothing? Look how the lilies of the field grow; they neither toil nor spin...Now if God so clothes the grass of the field which blooms to-day and is thrown to-morrow into the furnace, will not he much more clothe you? O men, how little you trust him!...(Pagans make all that their aim in life) for well your heavenly Father knows you need all that. Seek God's Realm and his goodness, and all that will be yours over and above.

NEB—'Therefore I bid you put away anxious thoughts about food and drink to keep you alive, and clothes to cover your body. Surely life is more than food, the body more than clothes. Look at the birds of the air; they do not sow and reap and store in barns, yet your heavenly Father feeds them. You are worth more than the birds!...And why be anxious about clothes? Consider how the lilies grow in the fields; they do not work, they do not spin...But if that is how God clothes the grass in the fields, which is there today, and tomorrow is thrown on the stove, will he not all the more clothe you? How little faith you have!...All these are things for the heathen to run after, not for you, because your heavenly Father knows that you need them all. Set your mind on God's kingdom and his justice before everything else, and all the rest will come to you as well.'

1 Corinthians 13:3
And though I bestow all my goods to feed the poor, and though I give my body to be burned, and have not charity, it profiteth me nothing.

Amp—Even if I dole out all that I have [to the poor in providing] food, and if I surrender my body to be burned [or in order that I may glory], but have not love [God's love in me], I gain nothing.

Mof—I may distribute all I possess in charity, I may give up my body to be burnt, but if I have no love, I make nothing of it.

NEB—I may dole out all I possess, or even give my body to be burnt, but if I have no love, I am none the better.

Romans 13:7,8
Render therefore to all their dues: tribute to whom tribute is due; custom to whom custom; fear to whom fear; honour to whom honour. Owe no man any thing, but to love one another: for he that loveth another hath fulfilled the law.

Amp—Render to all men their dues. [Pay] taxes to whom taxes are due, revenue to whom revenue is due, respect to whom respect is due, and honor to whom honor is due. Keep out of debt and owe no man anything, except to love one another; for he who loves his neighbor—who practices loving others—has fulfilled the Law [relating to one's fellowmen], meeting all its requirements.

Mof—Pay them all their respective dues, tribute to one, taxes to another, respect to this man, honour to that, Be in debt to no man—apart from the debt of love one to another. He who loves his fellow-man has fulfilled the law.

NEB—Discharge your obligations to all men; pay tax and toll, reverence and respect, to those to whom they are due. Leave no claim outstanding against you, except that of mutual love. He who loves his neighbour has satisfied every claim of the law.

1 Timothy 6:17-19

Charge them that are rich in this world, that they be not highminded, nor trust in uncertain riches, but in the living God, who giveth us richly all things to enjoy; That they do good, that they be rich in good works, ready to distribute, willing to communicate; Laying up in store for themselves a good foundation against the time to come, that they may lay hold on eternal life.

Amp—As for the rich in this world, charge them not to be proud and arrogant and contemptuous of others, nor to set their hopes on uncertain riches but on God, Who richly and ceaselessly provides us with everything for [our] enjoyment; [Charge them] to do good, to be rich in good works, to be liberal and generous-hearted, ready to share [with others], In this way laying up for themselves [the riches that endure forever] a good foundation for the future, so that they may grasp that which is life indeed.

Mof—Charge the rich of this world not to be supercilious, and not to fix their hopes on so uncertain a thing as riches but on the living God who richly provides us with all the joys of life; bid them be bountiful, rich in good works, open-handed and generous, amassing right good treasure for themselves in the world to come, so as to secure the life which is life indeed.

NEB—Instruct those who are rich in this world's goods not to be proud, and not to fix their hopes on so uncertain a thing as money, but upon God, who endows us richly with all things to enjoy. Tell them to do good and to grow rich in noble actions, to be ready to give away and to share, and so acquire a treasure which will form a good foundation for the future. Thus they will grasp the life which is life indeed.

Matthew 6:19-21
Lay not up for yourselves treasures upon earth, where moth and rust doth corrupt, and where thieves break through and steal: But lay up for yourselves treasures in heaven, where neither moth nor rust doth corrupt, and where thieves do not break through nor steal: For where your treasure is, there will your heart be also.

Amp—Do not gather and heap up and store for yourselves treasures on earth, where moth and rust and worm consume and destroy, and where thieves break through and steal; But gather and heap up and store for yourselves treasures in heaven, where neither moth nor rust nor worm consume and destroy, and where thieves do not break through and steal;

For where your treasure is, there will your heart be also.

Mof—Store up no treasures for yourself on earth, where moth and rust corrode, where thieves break in and steal: store up treasures for yourselves in heaven, where neither moth nor rust corrode, where thieves do not break in and steal. For where your treasure lies, your heart will lie there too.

NEB—Do not store up for yourselves treasure on earth, where it grows rusty and moth-eaten, and thieves break in to steal it. Store up treasure in heaven, where there is no moth and no rust to spoil it, no thieves to break in and steal. For where your treasure is, there will your heart be also.

Luke 16:10-12
He that is faithful in that which is least is faithful also in much: and he that is unjust in the least is unjust also in much. If therefore ye have not been faithful in the unrighteous mammon, who will commit to your trust the true riches? And if ye have not been faithful in that which is another man's, who shall give you that which is your own?

Amp—He who is faithful in a very little [thing], is faithful also in much; and he who is dishonest and unjust in a very little [thing], is dishonest and unjust also in much. Therefore, if you have not been faithful in the [case of] the unrighteous mammon—the deceitful riches, money, possessions—who will entrust to you the true riches? And if you have not proved faithful in that which belongs to another [whether God or man], who will give you that which is your own [that is, the true riches]?

Mof—He who is faithful with a trifle is also faithful with a large trust, and he who is dishonest with a trifle is also dishonest with a large trust. So if you are not faithful with dishonest mammon, how can you ever be trusted with true Riches? And if you are not faithful with what belongs to another, how can you ever be given what is your own?

NEB—The man who can be trusted in little things can be trusted also in great; and the man who is dishonest in little things is dishonest also in great things. If, then, you have not proved trustworthy with the wealth of this world, who will trust you with the wealth that is real? And if you have proved untrustworthy with what belongs to another, who will give you what is your own?

Philippians 4:19
But my God shall supply all your need according to his riches in glory by Christ Jesus.

Amp—And my God will liberally supply (fill to the full) your every need according to His riches in glory in Christ Jesus.

Mof—My God will supply all your own needs from his wealth in Glory in Christ Jesus.

NEB—And my God will supply all your wants out of the magnificence of his riches in Christ Jesus.

Mark 10:29,30

And Jesus answered and said, Verily I say unto you, There is no man that hath left house, or brethren, or sisters, or father, or mother, or wife, or children, or lands, for my sake, and the gospel's, But he shall receive an hundredfold now in this time, houses, and brethren, and sisters, and mothers, and children, and lands, with persecutions; and in the world to come eternal life.

Amp—Jesus said, Truly, I tell you, there is no one who has given up and left house or brothers or sisters or mother or father or children or lands, for My sake and for the Gospel, Who will not receive a hundred times as much now in this time, houses and brothers and sisters and mothers and children and lands, with persecutions, and in the age to come eternal life.

Mof—Jesus said, ''I tell you truly, no one has left home or brothers or sisters or mother or father or children or lands for my sake and for the sake of the gospel, who does not get a hundred times as much—in this present world homes, brothers, sisters, mothers, children and lands, together with persecutions, and in the world to come life eternal.''

NEB—Jesus said, 'I tell you this: there is no one who has given up home, brothers or sisters, mother, father or children, or land, for my sake and for the Gospel, who will not receive in this age a hundred times as much— houses, brothers and sisters, mothers and children, and land—and persecutions besides; and in the age to come eternal life.'

Mark 4:23-29
If any man have ears to hear, let him hear. And he said unto them, Take heed what ye hear: with what measure ye mete, it shall be measured to you: and unto you that hear shall more be given. For he that hath, to him shall be given: and he that hath not, from him shall be taken even that which he hath. And he said, So is the kingdom of God, as if a man should cast seed into the ground; And should sleep, and rise night and day, and the seed should spring and grow up, he knoweth not how. For the earth bringeth forth fruit of herself; first the blade, then the ear, after that the full corn in the ear. But when the fruit is brought forth, immediately he putteth in the sickle, because the harvest is come.

Amp—If any man has ears to hear, let him be listening, and perceive and comprehend. And He said to them, Be careful what you are hearing. The measure [of thought and study] you give [to the truth you hear] will be the measure [of virtue and knowledge] that comes back to you, and more [besides] will be given to you who hear. For to him who has will more be given, and from him who has nothing, even what he has will be taken away (by force), And He said, The kingdom of God is like a man who scatters seed upon the ground, Then continues sleeping and rising night and day while the seed sprouts and grows and increases, he knows not how. The earth produces [acting] by itself, first the blade, then the ear, then the full grain in the ear. But when the grain is ripe and permits, immediately he sends forth [the reapers] and puts in the sickle, because the harvest stands ready.

Mof—If anyone has an ear to hear, let him listen to this. Also he said to them, ''Take care what you hear; the measure you deal out to others will be dealt out to yourselves, and you will receive extra. For he who has, to him shall more be given; while as for him who has not, from him shall be taken even what he has.'' He said, ''It is with the Realm of God as when a man has sown seed on earth; he sleeps at night and rises by day, and the seed sprouts and shoots up—he knows not how. (For the earth bears crops by itself, the blade first the ear of corn next, and then the grain full in the ear.) But whenever the crop is ready, he has the sickle put in at once, as harvest has come.''

NEB—If you have ears to hear, then hear. He also said, 'Take note of what you hear; the measure you give is the measure you will receive, with something more besides. For the man who has will be given more, and the man who has not will forfeit even what he has.' He said, 'The kingdom of God is like this. A man scatters seed on the land; he goes to bed at night and gets up in the morning, and the seed sprouts and grows—how, he does not know. The ground produces a crop by itself, first the blade, then the ear, then fullgrown corn in the ear; but as soon as the crop is ripe, he plies the sickle, because harvest-time has come.'

2 Chronicles 26:5
And he sought God in the days of Zechariah, who had understanding in the visions of God: and as long as he sought the Lord, God made him to prosper.

Amp—He set himself to seek God in the days of Zechariah who instructed him in the things of God; and as long as he sought [inquired of, yearned for] the Lord, God made him prosper.

Mof—He steadily worshipped God during the lifetime of Zechariah, who gave instruction in religion, and as long as he worshipped the Eternal, God gave him success.

NEB—He set himself to seek the guidance of God in the days of Zechariah, who instructed him in the fear of God; as long as he sought guidance of the Lord, God caused him to prosper.

2 Chronicles 31:21

And in every work that he began in the service of the house of God, and in the law, and in the commandments, to seek his God, he did it with all his heart, and prospered.

Amp—And every work that he began in the service of the house of God, in keeping with the law and the commandments to seek his God, inquiring of and yearning for Him, he did with all his heart, and prospered.

Mof—Whatever he undertook in the interests of the temple of God, the law, and the commands of God, by way of worshipping his God, he did it with all his heart, and prospered.

NEB—Whatever he undertook in the service of the house of God and in obedience to the law and the commandment to seek guidance of his God, he did with all his heart, and he prospered.

2 Kings 18:7

And the Lord was with him; and he prospered whithersoever he went forth: and he rebelled against the king of Assyria, and served him not.

Amp—And the Lord was with Hezekiah; he prospered wherever he went. And he rebelled against the king of Assyria and refused to serve him.

Mof—And the Eternal was on his side; wherever he made an expedition, he succeeded. He rebelled against the king of Assyria and refused to serve him.

NEB—So the Lord was with him and he prospered in all that he undertook; he rebelled against the king of Assyria and was no longer subject to him.

Isaiah 48:15,17
I, even I, have spoken; yea, I have called him: I have brought him, and he shall make his way prosperous...Thus saith the Lord, thy Redeemer, the Holy One of Israel; I am the Lord thy God which teacheth thee to profit, which leadeth thee by the way that thou shouldest go.

Amp— I, even I, have foretold it; yes, I have called him [Cyrus]; I have brought him, and the Lord shall make his way prosperous... Thus says the Lord, your Redeemer, the Holy One of Israel: I am the Lord your God who teaches you to profit, Who leads you by the way that you should go.

Mof—I foretold it, 'twas I called him, 'twas I brought him, I have prospered him...This is the word of the Eternal your deliverer, the Majestic One of Israel: I am the Eternal your God, training you for your good, leading you by the right way.

NEB—I, I myself, have spoken, I have called him, I have made him appear, and wherever he goes he shall prosper...Thus says the Lord your ransomer, the Holy One of Israel: I am the Lord your God: I teach you for your own advantage and lead you in the way you must go.

Deuteronomy 30:19,20
I call heaven and earth to record this day against you, that I have set before you life and death, blessing and cursing: therefore choose life, that both thou and thy seed may live: That thou mayest love the Lord thy God, and that thou mayest obey his voice, and thou mayest cleave unto him: for he is thy life, and the length of thy days: that thou mayest dwell in the land which the Lord sware unto thy fathers, to Abraham, to Isaac, and to Jacob, to give them.

Amp—I call Heaven and earth to witness this day against you, that I have set before you life and death, the blessing and the curse; therefore choose life, that you and your descendants may live; To love the Lord your God, to obey His voice, and to cling to Him; for He is your life, and the length of your days, that you may dwell in the land which the Lord swore to give to your fathers, to Abraham, Isaac, and Jacob.

Mof—Here and now I call heaven and earth to witness against you that I have put life and death before you, the blessing and the curse: choose life, then, that you and your children may live, by loving the Eternal your God, obeying his voice, and holding fast to him, for that means life to you and length of days, that you may live in the land which the Eternal swore to Abraham, Isaac, and Jacob, your fathers, that he would give to them.

NEB—I summon heaven and earth to witness against you this day: I offer you the choice of life or death, blessing or curse. Choose life and then you and your descendants will live; love the Lord your God, obey him and hold fast to him: that is life for you and length of days in the land which the Lord swore to give to your forefathers, Abraham, Isaac and Jacob.

2 Corinthians 8:9
For ye know the grace of our Lord Jesus Christ, that, though he was rich, yet for your sakes he became poor, that ye through his poverty might be rich.

Amp—For you are coming progressively to be acquainted with and to recognize more strongly and clearly the grace of our Lord Jesus Christ—His kindness, His gracious generosity, His undeserved favor and spiritual blessing; [in] that though He was [so very] rich, yet for your sakes He became [so very] poor, in order that by His poverty you might become enriched—abundantly supplied.

Mof—You know how gracious our Lord Jesus Christ was; rich though he was, he became poor for the sake of you, that by his poverty you might be rich.

40

NEB—For you know how generous our Lord Jesus Christ has been: he was rich, yet for your sake he became poor, so that through his poverty you might become rich.

Deuteronomy 28:1,2

And it shall come to pass, if thou shall hearken diligently unto the voice of the Lord thy God, to observe and to do all his commandments which I command thee this day, that the Lord thy God will set thee on high above all nations of the earth: And all these blessings shall come on thee, and overtake thee, if thou shalt hearken unto the voice of the Lord thy God.

Amp—If you will listen diligently to the voice of the Lord your God, being watchful to do all His commandments which I command you this day, the Lord your God will set you high above all the nations of the earth, And all these blessings shall come upon you and overtake you, if you heed the voice of the Lord your God.

Mof—If only you will listen carefully to what the Eternal your God orders, mindful to carry out all his commands which I enjoin upon you this day, then the Eternal your God will lift you high above all the nations of the earth, and all these blessings shall come upon you and overtake you, if only you listen to the voice of the Eternal your God.

NEB—If you will obey the Lord your God by diligently observing all his commandments

which I lay upon you this day, then the Lord
your God will raise you high above all nations
of the earth, and all these blessings shall come
to you and light upon you, because you obey
the Lord your God.

Galatians 3:13,14
**Christ hath redeemed us from the curse of the
law, being made a curse for us: for it is written, Cursed is everyone that hangeth on a
tree: That the blessing of Abraham might
come on the Gentiles through Jesus Christ;
that we might receive the promise of the
Spirit through faith.**

Amp—Christ purchased our freedom (re-
deeming us) from the curse (doom) of the
Law's (condemnation), by [Himself] becoming
a curse for us, for it is written [in the Scrip-
tures], Cursed is everyone who hangs on a
tree (is crucified); To the end that through
[their receiving] Christ Jesus, the blessing
[promised] to Abraham might come upon the
Gentiles, so that we through faith might [all]
receive [the realization of] the promise of the
(Holy) Spirit.

Mof—Christ ransomed us from the curse of
the Law by becoming accursed for us (for it is
written, Cursed is everyone who hangs on a
gibbet), that the blessings of Abraham might
reach the Gentiles in Christ Jesus, so that by
faith we might receive the promised Spirit.

NEB—Christ bought us freedom from the
curse of the law by becoming for our sake an

accursed thing; for Scripture says, 'A curse is on everyone who is hanged on a gibbet.' And the purpose of it all was that the blessings of Abraham should in Jesus Christ be extended to the Gentiles, so that we might receive the promised Spirit through faith.

Ephesians 4:28
Let him that stole steal no more: but rather let him labour, working with his hands the thing which is good, that he may have to give to him that needeth.

Amp—Let the thief steal no more, but rather let him be industrious, making an honest living with his own hands, so that he may be able to give to those in need.

Mof—Let the thief steal no more; rather let him work and put his hands to an honest task, so as to have something to contribute to the needy.

NEB—The thief must give up stealing, and instead work hard and honestly with his own hands, so that he may have something to share with the needy.

Luke 7:23
And blessed is he, whosoever shall not be offended in me.

Amp—And blessed—happy [with lifejoy and satisfaction in God's favor and salvation apart from outward conditions] and to be envied—is he who takes no offense in Me and who is not hurt or resentful or annoyed or repelled or made to stumble, [whatever may occur].

Mof—And blessed is he who is repelled by nothing in me!

NEB—And happy is the man who does not find me a stumbling-block.

Haggai 2:7-9
And I will shake all nations, and the desire of all nations shall come: and I will fill this house with glory, saith the Lord of hosts. The silver is mine, and the gold is mine, saith the Lord of hosts. The glory of this latter house shall be greater than of the former, saith the Lord of hosts: and in this place will I give peace, saith the Lord of hosts.

Amp—And I will shake all nations, and the desire and the precious things of all nations shall come in, and I will fill this house with splendor, says the Lord of hosts. The silver is Mine, and the gold is Mine, says the Lord of hosts. The latter glory of this house [with its successor, to which Jesus came] shall be greater than the former, says the Lord of hosts; and in this place will I give peace and prosperity, says the Lord of hosts.

Mof—Very soon I will be shaking the sky, the earth, the sea, and the dry land, and shaking all nations till the treasures of all nations are brought hither and my House here filled with splendour (says the Lord of hosts). Mine is the silver, mine the gold, the Lord of hosts declares; the later splendour of this House shall outshine the former (says the Lord of hosts), and I will make this place prosper, says the Lord of hosts.

NEB—I will shake all nations; the treasure of all nations shall come hither, and I will fill this house with glory; so says the Lord of Hosts. Mine is the silver and mine the gold, says the Lord of Hosts, and the glory of this latter house shall surpass the glory of the former, says the Lord of Hosts. In this place will I grant prosperity and peace. This is the very word of the Lord of Hosts.

Mark 4:20-25
And these are they which are sown on good ground; such as hear the word, and receive it, and bring forth fruit, some thirtyfold, some sixty, and some an hundred. And he said unto them, Is a candle brought to be put under a bushel, or under a bed? and not to be set on a candlestick? For there is nothing hid, which shall not be manifested; neither was any thing kept secret, but that it should come abroad. If any man have ears to hear, let him hear. And he said unto them, Take heed what ye hear: with what measure ye mete, it shall be measured to you: and unto you that hear shall more be given. For he that hath, to him shall be given: and he that hath not, from him shall be taken even that which he hath.

Amp—And those that were sown on the good (well-adapted) soil are the ones who hear the Word, and receive and accept and welcome it and bear fruit, some thirty times as much as was sown, some sixty times as much, and some [even] a hundred times as much. And He said to them, Is the lamp brought in to be put under a peckmeasure, or under a bed, and not on the [lamp] stand? Things are hidden [temporarily] only as a means to revelation. For there is nothing hidden except to be revealed, nor is anything [temporarily] kept secret except in order that it may be made known. If any man has ears to hear, let him be listening, and perceive and comprehend. And He said to them, Be careful what you are hearing. The measure [of thought and study] you give [to the truth you hear] will be the measure [of virtue and knowledge] that comes back to you, and more [besides] will be given to you who hear. For to him who has will more be given, and from him who has nothing, even what he has will be taken away (by force).

Mof—As for those who were sown 'on good soil,' these are the people who listen to the word and take it in, bearing fruit at the rate of thirty, sixty, and a hundredfold. He also said to them, "Is a lamp brought to be placed under a bowl or a bed? Is it not to be placed upon the stand? Nothing is hidden except to be disclosed, nothing concealed except to be revealed. If anyone has an ear to hear, let him listen to this." Also he said to them, "Take care what you hear; the measure you deal out

46

to others will be dealt out to yourselves, and you will receive extra. For he who has, to him shall more be given; while as for him who has not, from him shall be taken even what he has.''

NEB—And there are those who receive the seed in good soil; they hear the word and welcome it; and they bear fruit thirtyfold, sixtyfold, or a hundredfold. He said to them, 'Do you bring in the lamp to put it under the meal-tub, or under the bed? Surely it is brought to be set on the lamp-stand. For nothing is hidden unless it is to be disclosed, and nothing put under cover unless it is to come into the open. If you have ears to hear, then hear.' He also said, 'Take note of what you hear; the measure you give is the measure you will receive, with something more besides. For the man who has will be given more, and the man who has not will forfeit even what he has.'

Joshua 1:5
There shall not any man be able to stand before thee all the days of thy life: as I was with Moses, so I will be with thee: I will not fail thee, nor forsake thee.

Amp—No man shall be able to stand before you all the days of your life. As I was with Moses, so I will be with you; I will not fail you or forsake you.

Mof—Not a man shall be able to hold his own against you all the days of your life; as I was with Moses, so I will be with you; I will never fail you nor forsake you.

NEB—No one will ever be able to stand against you: as I was with Moses, so will I be with you; I will not fail you or forsake you.

Books by Kenneth Copeland

* The Force of Faith
* The Force of Righteousness
  The Troublemaker
  The Laws of Prosperity
  Our Covenant with God
  The Decision is Yours
* Welcome to the Family
* A Ceremony of Marriage
  You are Healed
  The Power of the Tongue
  Now are We in Christ Jesus
  Freedom from Fear
  Walking in the Realm of the Miraculous
* Prayer: Your Foundation for Success
  Outpouring of the Spirit
* Sensitivity of Heart

* Available in Spanish

Books by Gloria Copeland

* God's Will for You
  God's Will for Your Healing
* God's Will is Prosperity
* And Jesus Healed Them All
  Walk in the Spirit

* Available in Spanish

World Offices
of
Kenneth Copeland Ministries

UNITED STATES
Fort Worth, Texas 76192

ENGLAND
P.O. Box 15
Bath, BA1 1GD

PHILIPPINES
Box 2067
Manila 2800

SOUTH AFRICA
P.O. Box 50830
Randburg 2125

AUSTRALIA
Private Bag 2
Randwick, N.S.W. 2031
Sydney

CANADA
P.O. Box 58248
Vancouver, BC V6P 6K1

HONG KONG
P.O. Box 73003
Kowloon, Central Post Office

More Information

For a complete catalog of books, teaching tapes and records, write:

Kenneth Copeland Ministries
Fort Worth, Texas 76192